Well done!

I said Thank You

I can say Please!

It's right to be polite!

Manners Stickers

It's right to be polite!

I can say Thank You

I said Please

I've been polite today

D0009137

This book belongs to:

....

....

Written by Jillian Harker
Illustrated by Rachael O'Neill

This edition published by Parragon Books Ltd in 2015
and distributed by

Parragon Inc.
440 Park Avenue South, 13th Floor
New York, NY 10016
www.parragon.com

ISBN 978-1-4748-0341-0

Printed in China

Please!
Thank You!

PaRragon

Bath • New York • Cologne • Melbourne • Delhi
Hong Kong • Shenzhen • Singapore • Amsterdam

Mind your child's manners!

It's important to start teaching good manners early so they become a habit for life. The stories in the MIND YOUR MANNERS! series are written to make learning good manners a positive experience.

Here are some of the ways you can help to make it fun:

* Find a quiet time to look at this story together and encourage your child to join in. The rhymes make the story easy to remember.

* After every question, talk about what you might say or do. Ask your child for suggestions. Joining in will help them to learn.

* Use the pages at the end of the story to check that your child understands when it is appropriate to use good manners. There's a reward star for every right answer.

* Throughout the day, reward your child's good manners with plenty of praise—and a colorful sticker.

When you want to join friends,
What do you say?
Do you cry and shout,
"I want to play!"?

That
can't
be
right!
It isn't
polite!

There's no need to be rude.
Here's the right thing to do:

First you say, "Please!"

And then say, "Thank you!"

"Here we go 'round the mulberry bush!"

If you're hot and you're thirsty
And want some ice cream,
Is the right way to get one
To stamp around and scream?

That can't be right!
It isn't polite!

There's no need to be rude.
Here's the right thing to do:

First you say, "Please!"

And then say, "Thank you!"

Yum, Yum!

If you need some help
To pedal along,
Do you say, "Push harder,
You're doing it wrong!"?

That
can't
be
right!
It isn't
polite!

There's no need to be rude.
Here's the right thing to do:

First you say, "Please!"

And then say, "Thank you!"

Vroom! Vroom!

If you fly your kite,
But it gets stuck in a tree,
Do you say, "Get my kite—
It's too high for me!"

That can't be right!
It isn't polite!

There's no need to be rude.
Here's the right thing to do:

First you say, "Please!"

And then say, "Thank you!"

If you want to be good
And have friends who will play,

Remember your manners—
It's better that way!

There's no need to be rude.
You know what to do: -

First we say, "Please!"

And then say, "Thank you!"

What will you say?

When you want to join friends, what will you say?

If you said "Please," you were right!

When you are given some ice cream, what will you say?

If you said "Thank you," you were right!

Did you say "Please" or "Thank you" in all the right places?
Then give yourself a star!

When you want some help,
what will you say?

If you said "Please," you were right!

When you get help,
what will you say?

If you said "Thank you," you were right!

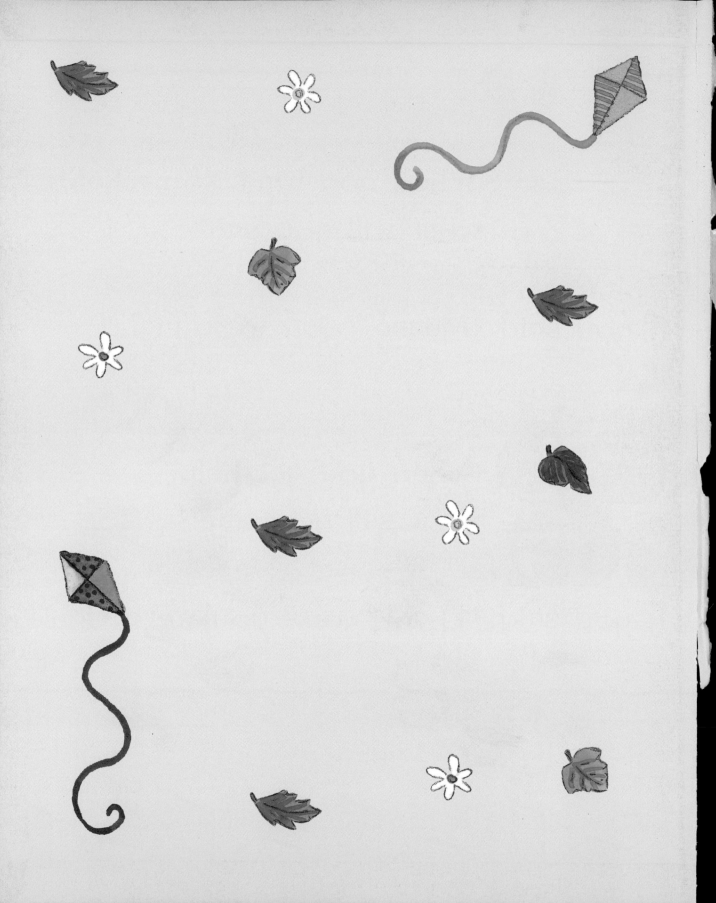